A Feeling of Poetry

Thoughts from the Inside

Dorian Frost

Cover Illustration by: Amy Smith

LitPrime Solutions
21250 Hawthorne Blvd
Suite 500, Torrance, CA 90503
www.litprime.com
Phone: 1 (209) 788-3500

© 2021 D.R.FROST. All rights reserved.

No part of this book may be reproduced, stored in a retrieval system, or transmitted by any means without the written permission of the author.

Published by LitPrime Solutions   06/29/2021

ISBN: 978-1-954886-48-3(sc)
ISBN: 978-1-954886-49-0(hc)
ISBN: 978-1-954886-50-6(e)

Library of Congress Control Number: 2021909461

Any people depicted in stock imagery provided by iStock are models, and such images are being used for illustrative purposes only.

Certain stock imagery © iStock.

Because of the dynamic nature of the Internet, any web addresses or links contained in this book may have changed since publication and may no longer be valid. The views expressed in this work are solely those of the author and do not necessarily reflect the views of the publisher, and the publisher hereby disclaims any responsibility for them.

Letter to the Reader ...

Dear readers,

A Feeling of Poetry is not your traditional poetry reading. Poetry is a form of art that often gets confusing in its meaning. From my original poetry book, *Feeling ... Thoughts from the Inside*, I wanted to express feeling in poem form.

Feeling is an emotion that often changes. Also, it can be expressed by putting yourself in the minds of others and things. What does it feel like to them or to the object to which we, as humans, relate?

What does it feel like to be in this area of distant space, as we relate with feeling in this case? I struggle to find my words to express the emotions that can put this question to rest.

But as you, the reader, explore and discover the area between my mind and emotion that is intertwined, I hope you can relate to me in some shape or design. The way we all think is just a sign.

When it is all said and done, I hope you can find the time to discover the feeling that each poem makes you feel—a feeling of poetry.

Here to express that feeling, I digress; below are the pages to explore. I rest. For on my table is the poetry on feeling and meaning, the ...

Table of Poetry

Letter to the Reader vii

Creativity 1
An Area of Distant Space.. 3
What Is Love? 7
Remember My Name 9
A Man... 11
A Feeling of Spring.. 13
A Wanderer Until … 17
The Rain Did Make a Sound... 21
Camp Hill.. 23
A Plan, across a Distant Land 27
My Mind Is Not Clear... 29
Frustration of the Grass 33
Smashed! 35
I Am the Storm 39
Frustrated! 43
Taken for Granted 45
Rain 47
Fear 49
It's Dark 51

Used and Abused	53
Drifting	55
I'm Different, You Fear	59
What He Could Be Thinking	63
Uncertainty	65
A Father Who Means So Much!	67
A Smile of Remembrance	69
African Traditions	73
A Valentine's Day Poem	79
Inspiration	81
Stand Up, Fill the Void	83
Depravity	85
Democracy	89
Depression Bites! But I pRaY!	95
Expressions	99
Author Description	101

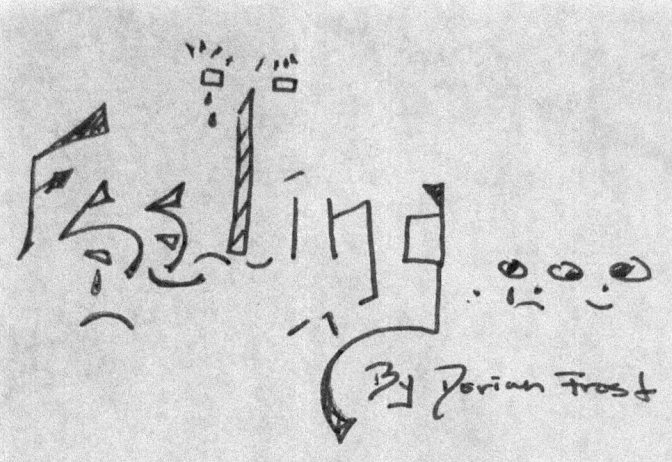

Creativity

A power one possesses in one's mind,
Creating things that are beyond time.

Different colors one imagines. Colors
of passion, emotion, and light
To which one can take flight.

In this moment of creative passion, we will
fly way across the blue-and-white sky.

Floating in this creative air, air that is never
dull or bare, we will create a rainbow in the
sky, one that will fly high and never die.

For creativity is what you and I make it, for
it is in one's mind that we design.
It is in one's mind that we wonder, in one's mind
that we can conjure things or objects that never
existed, in which some become realistic.

Creativity is a tool given to everyone, not just to some.
Used in many ways—whether in writing; making a book,
artistry, poems; building imagination—one can expound
on the world of fantasy, yet it can become reality.

Sharpen those skills by taking flight
Into the blue sky of creative oversight.

(Written in May 1998)

An Area of Distant Space

Looking up, I fathom the area of distant space,
For it's always there above my face.

Noticing a sun that is there,
which rises with its amazing glare.

A color, not of yellow but of light—light that blankets the sky and brings the colors of the world to life.

Let's be there in the sky,
Together, you and I.

Sometimes, I feel like the colors there.

In the mood of the shade of light,
In the colors that are warm and the colors that are cold,
I can feel warm, yet I can feel cold.

Yet even at night, my mind wanders with different feelings and emotions.

My mind takes flight
With the cold colors of black and white.

Oh, how they unite,
Making an awesome blue, these colors from the sky we call *night*.

A sky that is so pure,
Yet so true,
Even though it's cold and blue.

There is a glow from that sky,
That of objects that twinkle and shine.

From above, they pour down God's love.

Yet I feel the light.
It, too, is bright.

Just like the meaning of a Christian life.

It makes you stare in awe
As you smile at the wonders above that reflect his love.

Watch with a close eye; things can transpire within a moment or maybe even an hour.

Designs that spin the minds of people below,
Designs that we have come to know.

It's a whole world of shades and tints, making it different from the usual daily blue.
Yet this is the area that we call *night*, where things above our world begin to take flight.

However, as soon as night began, the sun begins to show its bright grin,
Its light, piercing away that of night, fading that of the world above, showing that area Atmosphere in which we only see with light.

It's amazing, that awesome blue, its color so rich and true.

A blue that is always there in the atmosphere,
Whether covered with rolling hills of gray or with hills of white—
Hills that form patterns and designs in the sky
That can look like a city when we fly.

Looking up, I can see the sky God created for you and me.

It's exciting to see the character of the air.

I feel like I'm there, in the air
When its air touches me with feeling.

Through seeing, I can watch the wind form swells in the sky
Or blow a tree down within a blink of an eye.

It roars and howls of an approaching storm.
Through the sounds and colors, you have been warned.

The colors of anger fill the sky with that of a blackish gray.

Excitement fills me from within
As I look out my window with a grin.

Just then, a strike of light spreads across the sky in an amazing sight.
A blast of BOOM and CRACKLE
Fills my ears as the sky pours down tears.

It's an atmosphere, an area of distant space,
An area you and I call sky; yes, that's the place.
A place that fills my mind with wonders
that I can not only see
But wonders I can feel,
Wonders that are real,
Wonders that are given by God's grace—
Grace that I'm able to see with my face.

Looking up, I fathom that area of distant space;
For it's always there above my face.

For after the storm, sometimes a rainbow is put in place,
Reminds me of my God and his promise,
For it is symbolic, of God's love and his amazing grace,
And that is that area of distant space.

What Is Love?

It's above me, what I can't understand, and that is love.
What is love?
Many people question,
But the truth is love soars high above our heads,
Higher than a flying dove.

My heart tears for it.
My heart longs for it.

Someone who cares, who can always be there.
Is it just the her or him and the always-be-there?

Or is it being near?
However, near is yet far.

People often use the phrase "make love,"
But it's like saying, "Let's make a dove."

My heart breaks; I cry.
My heart breaks; I sigh.
My heart breaks; I ask, "Why?"
My heart breaks into so many tears I make lakes.

Love can be full of pain,
Pain that will shower upon you like rain.

However, love can also feel good.
That is what we think it should.

However, the question still remains:
What is love?

What is love to me?
What is love to you?

Love to myself is so above me,
Above me that I can't even see.

Real love to me is still unknown.
Reason is it's more than companionship or relationship.

The kind of love that is known is that of the earth.
I've been experiencing this love since birth.

Love of the earth is that of acceptance,
Telling you that you're OK.

You are given this concept of fake love only through what others say.

But in reality, they, too, are lost with the same question:
What is real love?

Again, it's above them like a dove.
So can anyone answer the question, What is real love?

Remember My Name

People use me, thinking they know my purpose.
My mount is that of a flat surface.

People turn me with my purpose.

I am locked.
I am opened.
I am designed to perfection.

People grab me with the firmness of their hands,
Not paying any attention to the detail that I am.

Yes, I have a handle.
Yes, I have a name.

But most of my name was given
To the surface that I maintain.

Before the handle was the knob,
But I am one and the same.

Please, people, remember my name.
I am beaten; I am abused.
People pay no attention to my use.

But I am real, and I am here.
And without me, people will care.

Privacy is my main goal—
To give people what they need by doing what I am told.

So people, people, remember my name.
I am often colored gold,
But yes, a variety of shapes and sizes.
I am here when the sun rises.

I am around the world.

So people, remember my name.
I will be here even now,
And I will always, always be the same
Doorknob.

A Man

A man after his mother,
for this is what I am.

A man who wants to be
recognized as one, nothing other.

A man who wishes people would listen at times,
even when he did a crime.

A man with a wish for his mother
to see what he could be.

A man who wishes to be
part of his family.

A man who has a heart that cares,
wishing his mother would be there.

A man who has cried out to her in times of need.

A man who has been scared by rejection and her glee.

A man who wishes his mother would need him in her need.

A man who is ungrateful, for he has nothing to give his mom;
that is what she sees.

A man, though, who has fought the pain of realizing his wish
is too soon to come true.

A man who has fought through the pain of hate
to the joy of love.

A man who will rise up and say to this mom, "Just as God loved me."

For he was:

A man who had a wish for me to be what he knows I can be.

A man who was in pain when I was in the rain.

A man who cared enough to die
in order to bring life.

So in this, I say,
"In him is the way, and I want to be
a man from the sand, one who strives like my God;
in doing so, I can forgive and live."

In the end,

A man, one who loves God.

A Feeling of Spring

It's warm, the feeling
as I sit on this step.

It's amazing, the air
that rushes through my nose, a sneezing.

The sun's heat on my head,
making known its presence.

Looking up, I realize the hour of the day
as the sun beams straight down on me.

My mind is full of wonder as I look up at the world
that begins to show its color.

For it's spring, and things start to grow.

Things that are kind.
Things that blow your mind.

I watch a bee as I sit on my steps out in front of my house.
I watch as it buzzes around me.

I can almost feel the wind from its beating wings,
hearing the sound of the buzz it sings.
It's amazing to see the simple things around me.

To sit back and watch a tree.
Looking at a single branch with a bud of a seed,
I watch it sprout out a bead of green.

Then looking and seeing the trees together forming the green colors you and I see,
and that is spring.

Stop, look, and see the colors around thee.

Birds sing to me under the sun.
Looking, I watch them have fun.

Smelling grass that has been freshly mowed, the lines and patterns that it shows.

I begin to smile, for it brings me joy to see the things that God made right in my hand,
holding a flower that is part of God's master plan, or going to the beach and putting my feet in the sand.

Oh, how grand to be able to see the little things that he has done for me.

Yet spring is just one season, and there is a reason for everyone and everything; my God can do anything.

Sitting back, I like to feel my emotions that are real,
a feeling of spring, a joy of emotion God has given to me that I truly see.

A Wanderer Until …

Sweat drips off his forehead,
not being led.

For he struggles with a burden of sin, which has become that
of a huge weight he can't take.

Its chains weigh him down … dragging.
In desperation, he tries to find
another way to loosen the bind.

In doing so, they give him a name, a saying,
while others keep on praying,

A wanderer is his destination, is his name, if not to pursue
that path that is his imagination.

For there is a burnt image of a cross in his mind,
but he does not acknowledge this sign;
one would be blind.

Trying to find other ways of loosening the bind,
going to the cross, he does not.

Not taking the steps necessary,
given his excuses to carry, what he does with a *because*.

So, whatever now he carries,
he carries until …

His name will remain, and he will become the name, unless he fulfills the image,
which is against his will.
This will last to the end of this day unless he acknowledges the way.

Yes, a wanderer is what he has become; unless he acts against his will,
a wanderer he will remain until.

(Written in 1999)

Carrying his burden while thinking of the cross

The Rain Did Make a Sound

A roaring sound,
wind blowing around
as I watched, for in many different styles did the cold rain
hit the ground.

As I drove in the mountains,
as I drove on route 68 toward Ohio,
as I drove over many hills, up and down.

The rain often didn't make a sound
through thick bellows of fog all around.

Yet it did come with a blast and a sound.
My heart began to pound.

Eighty miles per hour I was driving; thick powder of misty
rain sprayed up harshly from the tires of the cars around;
this I found.

My music was loud,
for I was trying to remain calm
as the rain came down.

Struggling to see the truck in front of me
made it almost impossible for me to see.

Rain was all around,
blowing and smacking my windows, with that frightening howling sound.
Yes, that rain all hit the ground.

My heart began to pound.
Then I began to make a sound,
sing that of a Christian hymn,
which made me calm again.

But yes, after the fog came the rain, and then an awful sound.
After the rain was the fog, and it kept going around and around.
This, too, I found
as I drove in the mountains,
as I drove down route 68 toward Ohio,
as I drove over many hills, up and down.
Yes, it did make a sound, and it never stopped till the next day came around.
But that was the last thing I found on my trip over many hills, up and down,
for the rain did make a sound.

Camp Hill

Staring up across a green Camp Hill,
contemplating how I feel,
it's amazing to see a golden light
shine upon the green field of Hill
as the sun dissipates out of sight.

Just before the sun goes beyond my eyes,
I can see light gray smoke in different areas arise.

Smell of a camp flame fills my nose
more than the scent of a rose.

Sitting on top of it all,
watching my eyes fall

upon different camp flames here and there,
again I say, watching that smoke hit the air.

The sounds of people having fun,
enjoying the last moments in the sun.

My heart swells with excitement as I stare,
watching,
smelling,
being a part of camp that is there.

Oh, take the time to see the beauty that is around thee.

As I sit here and watch the golden light
roll off that hill,
my mind will always remember how I felt
about that Camp Hill.

For it was the beauty of the night after that golden light.
Stars began to fill that sky on Camp Hill.

Awe, what an awesome sight!
It made my spirit ignite.

Big Dipper,
Little Dipper,
and the Northern Star
near but yet so far.

Sitting on Camp Hill, looking up at a clearly seen Milky Way,
oh, how I wish I could stay.

Oh, what was that?
A shooting star,
going faster than a speeding car.

It's amazing to see
the things around thee.

Looking up at these white lights that really glow,
watching them light up Camp Hill below.

The green lawn turns to gray
as the light from the sky above sucks the color away.

Campfires here, down under that distant light,
make shadows on objects; what an amazing sight.

Smoke now you can only sense with your face,
and s'mores that are good to taste.

I say once again, from my spirit deep within,
my mind will always remember how I felt about that time I spent on that Camp Hill.

(Written in 2002 at Camp Andrews, Pennsylvania)

CAMP HILL

Stairring up Across a green
CAMP Hill
phantoming of How I feel.

Its amazing to See a Golden light
 Shone upon the Green, field
of Hill; As the Sun Disinpeares out
of Sight.

 Just before the Sun goes beyond
my eye's
 I could see light gray Smoke
in diffrent Area's Arise.

Smell of Camp flame fills my Nose
 More then the Sent of a Rose.

Sitting on top of it all,
 my eye's full.

A Plan, across a Distant Land

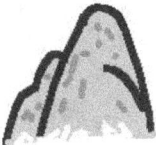

It takes you across the western plains;
it's something that I will try to explain.

From east and west it stretches;
from east to west it connects.

Its color is that of the night sky;
flowing across its flat surface makes me feel like I can fly.

It's fun to touch, thinking that with my light hand,
I have now been connected to every distant land.

Across every state,
even though its path is not straight.

But it's amazing, I say, to know that this thing is in front of thy face,
can take you to any place even within the states.

Color—with lines that divide and sometimes rails on either side—
on it, you can truly glide.
As I look up to the sky
on this curvy and sometimes straight surface,

I realize my life is that stretch of pavement, scoring across the land.
In my life, my pavement is set ahead of me like a plan,
yet it takes me anywhere; this I understand.

It's amazing to me to see and understand a road can take me across every stretch of naked land,
connecting me to people who I will soon come to understand,
and just like it is planned.

Just as things in my life are planned, I will travel as planned.
To travel across a distant land—
this I have come to understand.

(Written in 2003)

My Mind Is Not Clear

My mind, which is so near,
it's all but so clear.

Thinking of you,
dreaming of you.

This is a feeling that is so new.
What have you done to me,
setting me free?

Is this an emotion of love?
Can't be.

Yet I'm thinking of you nightly, and not just in the day,
thinking of you even though you're so far away.

My mind is all but empty with thoughts of you.

My dear,
you draw me near.

Full of these thoughts …
I crawl to you.
I can't help myself.

It's a feeling for you and no one else.
Thinking of you,
again and again,
you make my mind spin.

Talking on the phone, for you're a line away,
to go to you, this I pray.

I commit to you now, all but true.
Forever I long to be with you.
I don't speak that word of love,
for it's a word, and I feel the feeling of compassion,
something love can't touch.
I want to be with you so much.

Dreaming of you, we are together …

Holding hands, we walk under the shade of a tree.
We talk …
In my mind,
you are so kind,
you are my sign,
you are it all.
Together, we won't fall.

In my mind, it's full of thoughts unclear.
But one thing is …

Thinking of you,
dreaming of you,
I want to be with you,
for it's just me and you.

(Written in 2003)

Frustration of the Grass

Frustration of the grass—will it pass?

These blades shoot up and down.
Its green blades conquer my ground.
It's all around.

Twice a week, I mow,
but does it show?

No!

It gets on my clothes,
and it still grows,
even if I mow twice in a row.

Isn't it clear …
the frustrations I fear?

It gets in my nose,
making it drain like water coming out of a hose.

Achoo! I sneeze.
No tissue. I wipe it on my knees.

It grows and grows,
and I mow rows and rows!

Sweat comes down my face,
while the grass sticks to my shoelace.

Ah *no*! Not my face!
Will I ever win this race?

Even in between, I watch as it rains,
feeding that weed of green.
It's everywhere I have seen.

Ah! I grab my face
as I take the weed whacker; around the sidewalk edge I lace.

I say it grows and grows;
I mow rows and rows!

This is frustration of the grass; will it ever pass?

(Written in the summer of 2003 in Capitol Heights, Maryland)

Smashed!

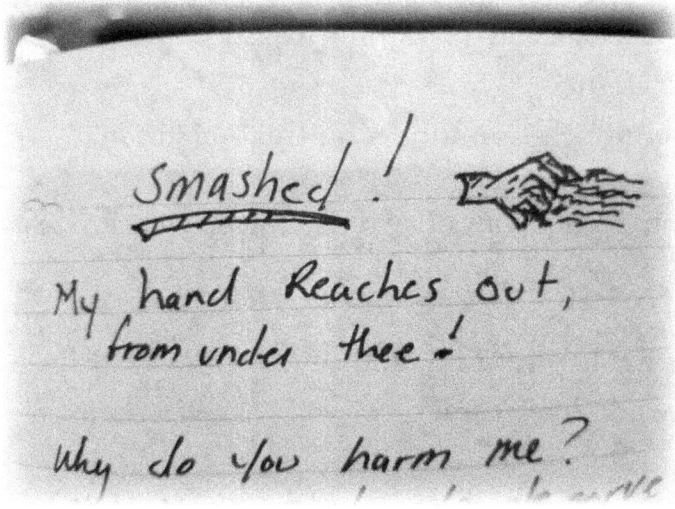

My hand reaches out
from under thee!

Why do you harm me?
What have I done to deserve?

This criminal that I am not!

I push up with my hand,
but like a wrench, it crushes down.

Pushing my soul, mind, and body into the ground,
my blood ran.

The pain starts with my head,
then goes through me and then:
my blood ran!

I grind my blackened hand in the sand,
trying to fight,
dragging myself from under all this weight.

I run into rather a lot of swords, then slowly am crushed by
the weight of emotions without cords.

It hurts my heart, mind, and soul
to be treated like a troll,
alien.

People don't understand
that we aren't all the same in this land.

What is the same for you?
It's not the same for me.

In reading, will not two people conjure a different meaning?

Crushed, smashed upon
because one has his own way of thinking.

Forced to take on the traits that are not of my own being.

I rather die, then cry,
taking on things that are not of my own seeing.

So, I've taken my other hand,
both now digging into the sand,
desperately crawling from under that death hand.
And my blood ran.
But I choose not to die in this sand; so what if my blood ran?

Being crushed, destroyed every day, smashed!
Smashed by death, I call it *hand*.

A hand that will crush you until you disregard the character of you.

My face twisted with anger,
my heart filled with fear,
I press on, but I am smashed once again with a single tear.

(Written in 2003, inspired by my being bullied)

I Am the Storm

Today, I am ripping up my walls.
Everything will fall.

It's a storm.
I am lightning.
I am the wind.
I am everything
within.

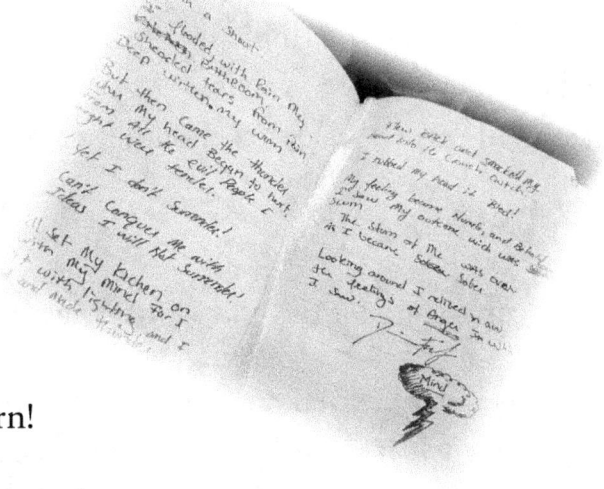

You came to my
home.
My curtains are torn!

I ripped them with wind
that came from within.

I call it a storm!

I will smack your mouth
with a bolt of lightning!

Don't talk to me. You're ugly.

Do you feel the fear?
Well, it's near!

I knocked my power out
with a shout.

I flooded with rain my bathroom,
shed tears from pain
deep within my wound.

But then came the thunder
when my head began to hurt
from all the evil people I thought were tender.

Yet I don't surrender!

You can't conquer me with your ideas; I will not surrender!

I will set my kitchen on fire with my mind!
For I struck it with lightning, and I screamed and made thunder.

Clap!

But it backfired and hit the stove, sending me flying higher.
I flew back and smacked my head into the couch ... *Ouch!*

I rubbed my head. It bled!

My feeling became numb,
and behold, I saw my outcome, which was scum.

The storm of me was over
as I became sober.

Looking around, I realized in awe the feeling of anger in which I saw.

(Written in 2003, with anger in my mind)

Frustrated!

Tipping my cup, the water ran,
ice sliding across the table.

My mind is not able.

My emotions moved so fast
they began to slip up.

Standing up, I can't take it.
I'm fired up.
Aggravation tipped my cup.

My focus lost!

This happens when I'm frustrated when things don't go right.

Frustrated!

If I miss my flight,

Frustrated!

When things end up in a mess,

Frustrated!

My mouth opens with a feeling of frustration,
a disease that carries from me to another, like a wave made by my constant vibration.
Arguments escalated by one vibration of frustration,
leaving me with another sense of frustration!

Taken for Granted

It's okay to have things a certain way,
but it's gone far beyond its case today.

It's the way in America we live our lives.
Without it, we would think we would die.

Our water has to be clear; even though it runs through our pipes and is clear,
no, can't drink that water at home. It's not pure.

Or a fly hits my plate and on my food—oh, how rude.
Ah! Fly, now if I eat that, I am going to die. Ugh! Fly, why?
Throw my food away, this I may.

Is this for real, how we think this way?
It is unreal how we take for granted the things around.

Back in the day,
people would die to live this way.

Question:
Did they have toilets that would run?
Question:
Could they watch a washing machine run just for fun?

Or
put a glass under the faucet for water and expect to get some?

Back in the day is when we didn't live that way.

An excuse I look at with dismay—
spoiled, we take for granted the way in which we live today.

We'd rather pay to live our way—for example, pay for water at the store, rather than grab it from home.
What for?
Or
buy another plate of food, rather than eat that which has been called on by a fly, for we could die!

It's okay to have things our certain way,
but not when it becomes the wasteful habit with which we live today.

(Written in 2002)

Rain

How does it make you feel,
the rain?

Me? It calms my veins ...

Everything is quiet in the storm.
Hard to describe its sound,
which calms my veins.

But it's that of the constant rain coming down.

My mind spins around and around.

My vision out the window is blurred by the lines of rain
coming down, forming a mear design across my picture frame.

It's exciting, yet I feel calm, as the rain keeps me sane.
It's amazing to see the rain
across my windowpane.

(Written in 2004)

Fear

It's in me sometimes;
I don't feel fine.

Something new, something different—
these are things that cause a feeling of fear.

Yet it's nothing; you don't shed tears.

It stops me from doing things.
Even stops people from getting that ring.
Because of the feeling, people think they can't sing.

For me, I get other feelings from fear,
ones that make my stomach do waves.
Or running to the bathroom,
or dropping serving trays, shaking,
stops me in the middle of a sentence,
or garbling up words.
But this is the second term that causes this to happen.

Afraid means *fear*, a feeling that I don't hold dear.

I am clumsy,
I am weak,

I am wanting to go to sleep,
I am lazy.

These things I am when I get afraid or fearsome,
but I just say tiresome
to express how I feel about the feeling of fear.

For in the feeling, that's not who I am,
the things I listed above, and because of this, I don't hold it dear.

The feeling of fear!

(Written in 2004)

It's Dark

It's dark; pick me up.
I lie sprawled on the floor.

Slam went the door, left alone on my own.

It's dark!

Lost in my mind, wandering.
Lost! It's dark.

Fear was creeping into my soul.
I'm going to die, I was told.

Silent was the noise.
Breathing, I felt from within
its denial; I am lost, it's silent,
it's dark!

I say in denial, for I am not lost in my mind, and there is light that blinds.
I say to myself,
But it's dark!

It's sin from within.
Cold, dark is the floor.

I reach for the door,
blood of me on the floor.

They hit me,
tried me,
made me weak.

It's dark!

Will I give up or fight?
Or should I say it's
dark?

For the sin in my life,
will you get up or fight
as I lie on the floor with that closed door?

(Written in 2004)

Used and Abused

Have I been used? Have I been abused?

Why do people take, take, take?
Don't ask; just take.

Assuming you will say yes,
don't bother to ask.

Have I been used or abused?

Society assumes a lot,
but is this right to assume we won't get shot?

It's okay to live this way, giving and expecting to receive.
But yes, it's okay to do something for another and expect thanksgiving.
Yet we will keep living.

Yes, this is a feeling of concern.

Yes, this is a feeling of anger!

I'm sure you assumed the rest, but is that the topic?
Let that put your mind to the test!

But the question still remains,
remains the same.

Have you been used, or have you been abused?

By assumption of your things,
by the demanding of our giving,
or by the expectation of your yes?

All I know is that the word *no*, which we have come to know little of,
is less and seldom used.

Lessened by the people who are often used,
for the answer is you don't use the word, so people walk all over you every time.

Yet you use it, and things will start to unwind,
feelings of anger and the reason why.
But it's hard on people's ears.

Can you stand on it?
Or will you be used and abused by the people you choose?

Drifting

How can a man affect me in a way that's hard to describe?
How can he cause me to lose my mind?
Do you realize how far it wanders,
wanting to imagine what my life would be like if you were near?

A man whom I never met but know!
A man who is always there when I need him most.
A man who understands me more than any other.
A man who wants me for who I am.
A man whose love is never questioned.

Drifting thoughts in my head putting me and you in a special place,
I find myself often now gazing into space.

A vision of you and me together,
oh, how I long to spend.
It will make me feel excited like summer.

Listening to your magic on CD,
you sweep me away with how you jam.

Can't you see how I long for thee?

Making me cry when you're not around when I am sad,
but also making me laugh when I am glad?

You have this power over me.
This I see, drifting thoughts in my head.

I want to be there for you when you cry.
I don't ever want to say good-bye.

I want to cook for you in our kitchen.
I want to paint the sky with our love,
play around like we are children.

I want to make you smile, make you cry, and make you mad.
I want you to show me your emotions.
I just want to know you,
more than anyone!

Making me think of you, more and more I drift
into a space where I feel safe—
drift into a place where it's you and that beautiful face.
You call me names, making my mind spin into a whirl of
things that make me smile.
Saying kinky things that make my temperature rise,
knowing what turns me on, you make my mind drift. Spill
out white spew from my insides,

making me scream, "I love you!"
How can you control me, drifting into a place I can't find, making me lost inside of you?

I want to hug, hold, and think of you.
I want to hug, hold, and feel you spanking me and saying things that make me drift, yet again into a place I love.

A place that only you have that key to unlock. Deep inside me, feeling me, holding me, kissing me, and rubbing me. Goddamn. You make my mind spin, and all is done without you even being near!

My mind drifting into lust,
my mind drifting into you!

(Written on March 18, 2005)

I'm Different, You Fear

You don't understand!
You think you know me.
You think you can put your finger on me.

What is your fear?
What is your reason for being here?
What is your goal for teasing me?

When I was a child,
when I was at school,
when I was an adult?

You don't understand!
You think you know me.
You think you can put your finger on me.

Why call me a name?
Why place my mind, spirit, and actions in a category?
Why tell me I'm different from you?

I know I'm different from most guys.
I know, I know I speak a little high.
I know my difference and my place in this world.

My mind hurts.

My soul has gone through pain.
My physical being has gone through the rain.

An adult now looking back, how I was slowly burned.
An adult now looking back, kids tore my dignity and showed me pain.
An adult now looking back, a result of the product of now!

Asking again, why put the remembrance before me?
Asking again, why bring up those emotions again?
Asking again, why cause me to feel the pain?

What have I done?
What do you want?
What can I give for you to let me live?

You don't understand; you're not God!

Yet you throw the law against me.
Yet, because I'm different from thee, I am the enemy.
Yet, now, I deserve to burn in hell.

Did I try to kill you?
Did I try to take thy children from you?
Did I hate on you, like you do me?

Tell me lies of God; don't love me.
Tell me lies that I am dirty.
Tell me lies that I'm not wanted.

Why do you fear?
Why are you here in front of me?
Why do you tease and treat me meanly?
You're not God!

(Written on February 17, 2006)

What He Could Be Thinking

Defined by his long beard and turban,

he stands on the rush-hour train, staring down.

There is no smile but a frown,
his culture defined by his blue hat, which is a turban.

I watch as he closes his eyes, wondering what he could be thinking.

In America now, I wonder,
Is he afraid of what people might think or say?

For with the things that have transpired, people look at him funny.
For his culture is thought of as a threat in today's society.

Look at him standing there with his hand on the bar,
his head down,
his mind wandering far,
but he must stand and be brave.

He is no terrorist; he is a citizen like you and I.
But an alien does he feel like, people looking, talking, and staring at him funny.

Yes, an alien he must feel like,
with the treatment of you and I.
It's sad to say that he may feel this way
standing on the train, thinking hard with his brain.

But America, oh yes, America, have we come a long way?

(Written on October 26, 2004)

Uncertainty

Tired is not what I would like to describe myself as at this moment, worn out by all the stuff that has gone around.

Looking inside,
Sitting on the ground, holding my knee, I'm not happy or full of glee.

Yet I'm not sad or angry or even mad.
Worn, from days of serving others, I feel lost, covered with something unseen.
Creative, something I feel inside has gone all, all but near me.
My spirit drags, deep inside.
Oh Lord, hear my cry!

Have I lost you? is my greatest fear!
Oh Lord, keep me near!

Not attending the fellowship I held dear,
My mind, my soul wonder.

Dark are the days of now,
Lots of people lost in the now.

Yet I look for my God once again,
And this is my poem's end.

(Written on September 28, 2005)

A Father Who Means So Much!

A Father's Day Poem ...

A father who means so much!
How do I express this!
A man, a father—a title that you have to be to understand?

To love, to care, understanding without understanding,
to provide advice even if he does not agree with choices made
by his children.

My dad has done so much,
understanding so much,
loving in a way that God does, unconditionally and
conditionally.

A tender heart, a spirit of joy, and a man I have come to
respect.
Even though we don't always agree, he is always there for me.

Listening and teaching every day,
there is much more to say.

A family man he is, always there, bringing joy when there is
pain, clarity to confusion,
asking God for the patience of which he has much.

Caring for his children he does well, guiding, leading even when we make him sad. That's my dad.

A man after God's own heart while being raised, seeing the struggle, seeing the strength that only God provides.

So how do I express this kind of man? Words don't quite grasp the emotion I feel. The happiness, the joy, the love, the tears that fill my eyes when I say I'm blessed with the kind of dad God blessed me with—it's a joyous realization.

Dad, more than a dad,
you're my friend who teaches, guides, leads, loves, cares, and is always there even when you're not.
I love you so very much. Happy Father's Day. You're the father who means so much!

A Smile of Remembrance

Dedicated to a hardworking grandma, one who is positive and very special to her grandkids

Sitting here on my steps, I am calm, putting all my thoughts aside.
It is here when you enter my head, so I take a moment of silence.

With the smile of remembrance on my face,
Grandma, you are special in my life, and in my heart, I hold a special place.

With conversations of love, and thoughts now of everything we share, guidance in your knowledge you bring into my life even when you're not there.

Among all the things I remember, most of all are the times we shared.
I could cry tears of joy for happiness when you are near.

"If you sprinkle when you tinkle"—this is a memory for me.
Oh, and yes, I will be a "sweetie and wipe the seattie."

Cream of chipped beef sparks a fire of compassion for you, and how you got up every morning to fix me a plate.

I couldn't count the love I have for you or even bring up a price or even a rate.

But yes, a special grandma to me—well, that just might sum it up.

Taught me to be me,
to follow my dreams,
to walk up straight, for God loves me.

Looking out in my mind, smiling at every memory past,
Grandma, you are a special one, indeed.

I'm glad my God gave you to me.

For I could look beyond the sea and still not find one as good as thee.

Recognizing things—that is important in my life now.
I'd rather have no money at all than give you up,
sausage, eggs, toast in the morning, and drinking orange
juice from a cup.

How you hated my storyline; it made me laugh when you
said it hurt your eyes to read my stuff.
But it's the little things like this that make me overcome
things that are tough.

Computer problems always bring us together, just as the
family problems do,
and I will always love you.

Everything is quiet; not even the birds do I hear. In remembrance
of you, I talk to you because I know you will hear.

Thank you, Grandma, for:

filling my cup when it was empty,
clothing me when I was naked,
feeding me when I was hungry,
and lifting my spirits when I was sad.

You are my grandma, whom no one can replace.
Amazing grace, how sweet the sound
that a grandma like you was found. You are the sweetest sound.
Greater than the greatest lake,

and a heart bigger than the biggest sea,
oh Grandma, oh, how I love thee.

Getting up now, I wear that smile, the smile of remembrance of a grandma who is good to me.

(Written on Mother's Day, 2015)

African Traditions

A school project

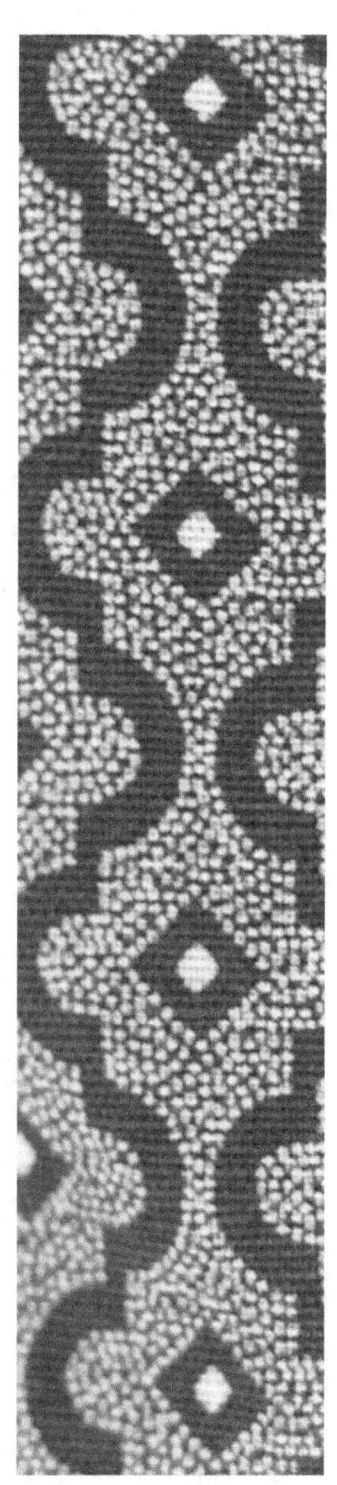

African traditions
Are affected by transitions,
Which turn and twist tribal positions.

For the white man and his God are coming,
Forcing new conditions,
Which the black man can't petition.

These new conditions

Bring about confusion to a black man's intuition.

Black men are forced to labor and are sent to an institution.

For a black man sent to an institution is forced to learn of the constitution and the white man's ways of persecution.

For African traditions
Are affected by transitions,

Which turn and twist tribal
positions.

African leaders are torn with
confusion
From the intrusion of the white
man's religion.

A circumcised female is considered
unholy in the white man's tradition.
However, black tribes see this as
disrespect, for a woman circumcised
is right in their tribal condition.

This is just one of the unseen ways
of tribal persecution,
The kind of persecution that
tortures a mind into a formal way of
retardation.

Children brought up in the old ways
of tribal legislation are forced into
the new, substantial, holy ways of the
white man's religion,
Of their new generation.

For African traditions
Are affected by transitions,
Which turn and twist tribal
positions.

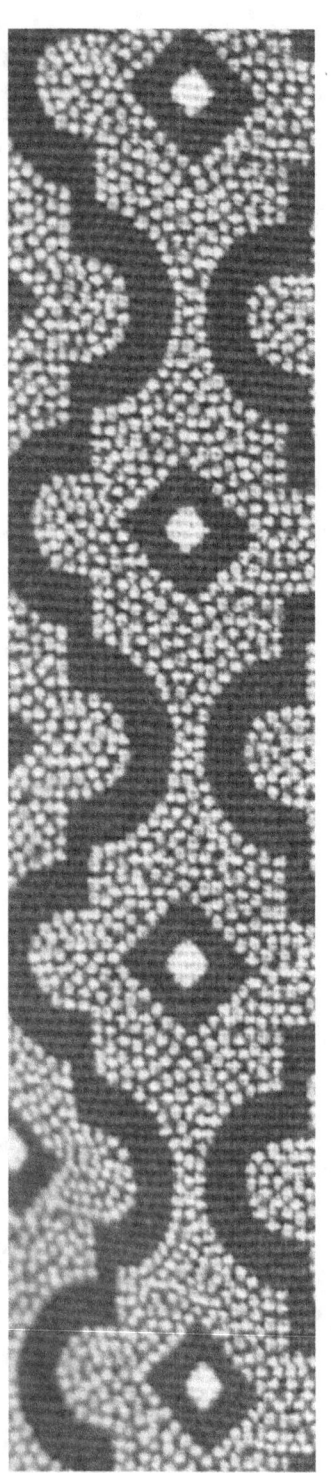

Names are reconditioned;
Names that once had a lot of recognition
Soon were taken, lessened.

For Europeans had no respect,
For ideas and dreams they could not detect.

Hearts were destroyed;
Evils were employed.

A black man's name soon was part of the white man's extradition,
Thus forcing the soul of the black man to a death-defying perdition.

African traditions
Were affected by transitions, which turn and twist tribal positions.
Regulations soon was forced on every black person in the African nation.

For stories of the white man's God were told;
His wonders of winning souls to Christ began to unfold.

Crushing the tribal legislation,

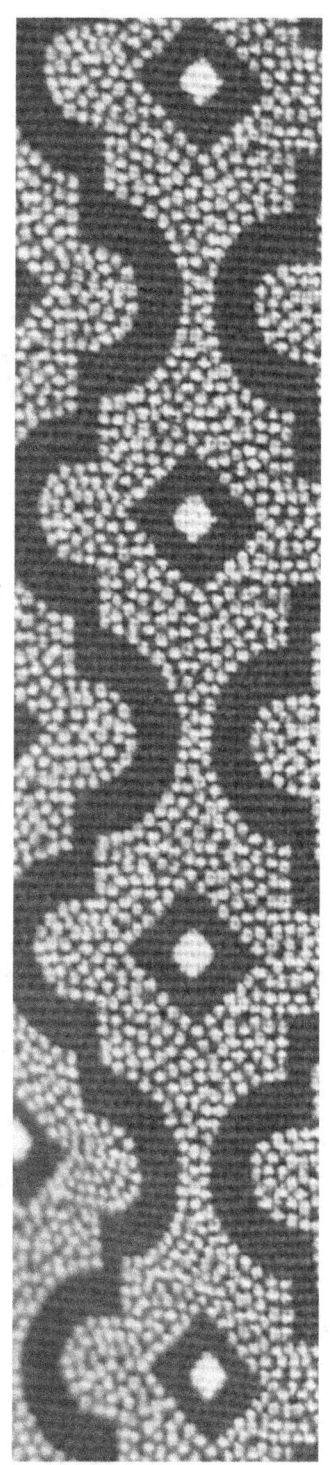

Pulling them to a proclamation.

Worriers started dissipation,
Which ended tribal legislation.

African traditions
Were affected by transitions,
Which turn and twist tribal positions.

White men gained a hold of conditions,
Started their own traditions.

Enslaving those who wanted to defy and make distractions,
With those who were in leadership with a new proclamation.

An old way of tradition
Soon became a distant figment of one's imagination.

Black people were soon confined,
Told to put their past and culture behind.

The result was their desolation.
Inside them, they felt as if wanting to start a revolution,

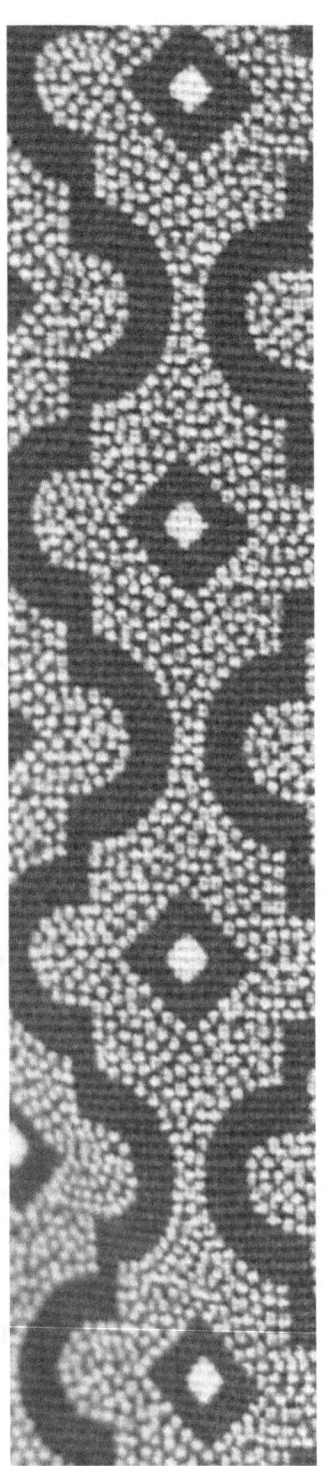

For they could not understand this resolution.

African traditions
Were affected by transitions,
Which turn and twist tribal positions.
The tribal village moved on in its desolate organizations.
However, taking a closer look, its culture still stands out, in a secret mess of organized solution.

Through all the massive persecution,
The tribe was able to overcome, withstand the European courts of Legalization
Though under European tradition.

European legislation repositioned blacks,
Who maintained their culture through racism and discrimination.

For African traditions
Were affected by transitions,
New legislations,
Which turned and twisted ancestors' positions.

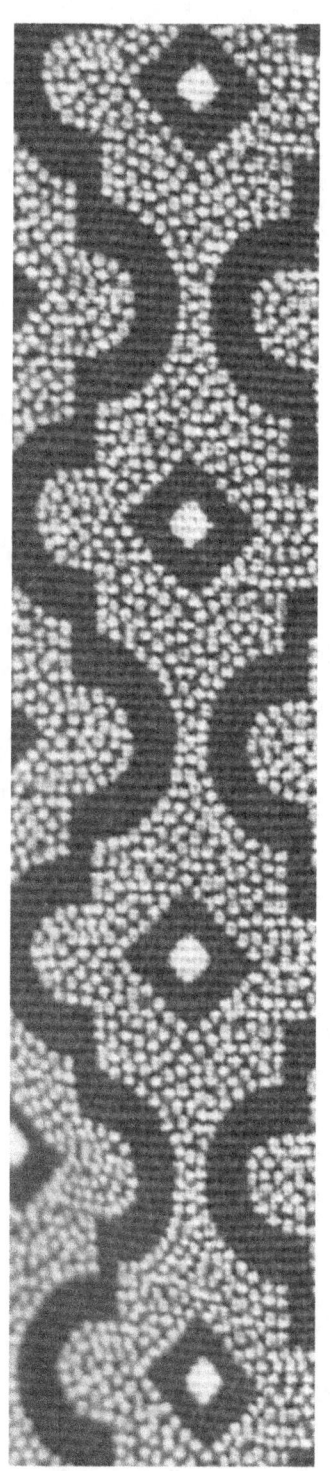

Yet it was not all lost,
Just repositioned with a cost.

Nevertheless, we survived the conditions
Of the white man's new religion.

When you see your friend or foe
On the street or on the door,

Remind him of our ancestors' tribal traditions,
How we survived on new conditions.

For African traditions
Are affected by transitions,
Which turn and twist tribal positions.

(Written on June 27, 2002, as a Black History class project)

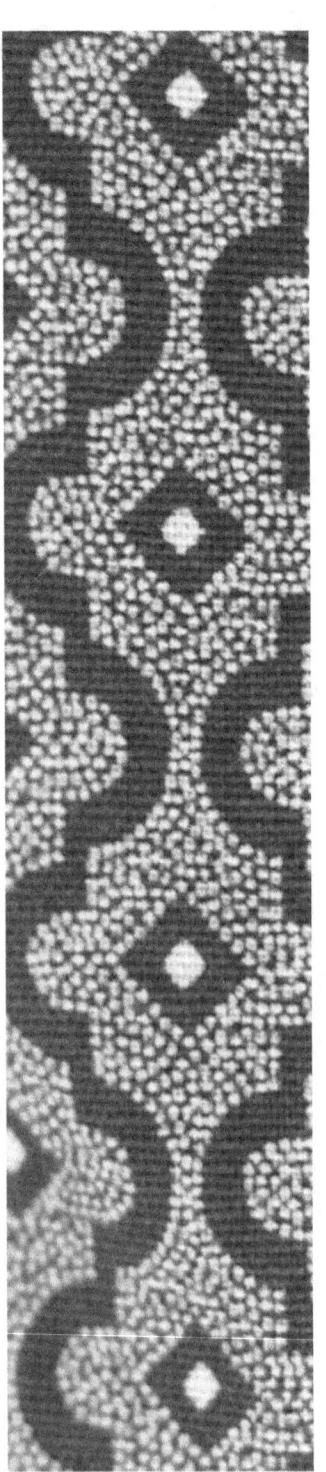

A Valentine's Day Poem

Would you be mine,
My valentine …

On a special day …

To share the love again or to begin again …
To listen, to embrace, to share face,

To cry tears of joy with someone
Or even to smile,

To laugh and to play.
Or to say …
Would you be mine,
My valentine?

To remember the good and the bad and be glad.
To embrace that we both, one another, race
and not waste the time we have.

Overall, I'm grateful to you and you to
me that we have each other.

Would you be mine again to go through life,
My valentine, that we can share, in
love, from now till the afterlife?

So would you be mine,
My valentine?

(Written on February 14, 2019)

Inspiration

A word that brings birth to creativity—
It is deep, this word of reactivity.

It excites me to see something so simple
Deep ... inside me.

Like wheels, my mind spins with emotion,
Desire to be more than simple motivation.

Simple inspiration sparks a burning flame
In others till it's an inferno who is to blame.

It's not just in song but in everything in being.
Just look around and see what's in front of thee.

A simple song or physical plan or even a book you read,
Inspiration—to get excited is to desire to find pleasure in the goal. Just get her done!

It's exciting to see that inspiration is part of me.

(Written on September 9, 2018)

Stand Up, Fill the Void

I don't declare more than I can see.
But to stand in the gap fills the void.

To understand truths, in fact, about yourself,
To recognize it's more about who you are …

Not the free sayers of the world,
Those dictators who speak to provoke
In selflessness, greed, not love.

Know thyself; speak up to those who ridicule.
Do I dare to be hidden and ashamed?

The Lord says *truth* … fearfully and wonderfully made.

Yet don't stay silent!
Kids, bullied, no activism, where are your rights?

Stand in that gap … Fill that void …

No hate, no suppression, no destruction.
Let it be you whose face is held high!

Standing in the gap fills the void!
You stand up for you! *I'll stand up for me.*

Together, we will bring unity!

Depravity

My heart is in a hole.
There was so much untold.

2017—a year of bad behavior, strife!
Blinded by greed, and what I want,
Yet who cares?

A whole lot of lying, deceit unleashed
By the Exxon CEO and his farce.

To our new president, oh yes, unmoral liar.
Trump, deceitful criminal.

My heart lashes out with anger, pain,
For others will soon suffer.

Wounded on a street with no bandage,
Hungry with no food to eat.

While a man stuffs his pockets with green while trampling
them with his government feet,
Muggles under the weight of the Voldemort wizard.

So much depravity … so much.

I look for days of old
To find a phoenix, born anew from the ash—
To see a country better than what it is now
To make our forefathers proud.

A dream

Of free health care,
A highway that does not rob you,
An airline that does not class you,
A bathroom to use because I have to go!

Help thy neighbor help thyself?
Morals ... morals, where are they? Where did you go?

One nation who stands on values would not stand for a president who lies ... talks about women ... does not take ownership of his actions but expects others to ... and deals with his own best interest while ignoring ours ... lies to you and lies to me ...

Can't you see?

My heart is in a hole ...
Sunken with sadness. It hurts!
I fall to my knees ... Lord, why?
I ask you?!

Is America lost … Can we turn a blind eye to the needy and be greedy?
Are we the terrorists to ourselves?
So much depravity, so much.
I can bear to watch …
History repeats … riots … racism … sexism … hate!
Is this our fate?
The word is only one:
Depravity!

Democracy

It's a democracy, a hypocrisy,
One that is subjected to its own end.

Where do I begin?

I could stand up and shout,
For now the government runs itself.

It's America, yes, America—one that holds its democracy high.
Yet its children cry.

It's the land of the free yes,
So it's supposed to be.

But it also is destined to end, if we don't defend.

A democracy whose government is composed of hypocrites of the nation of Christ,
Yet that is also a myth, soon to die.

A democracy that preached to every nation
With no limitation.

America, democracy given the right to police, with expectation
From other countries—
This has been going on for more than a century.

Yet out of control!

We are bold!

It's a democracy, a hypocrisy, one that cares for no men but
their money.
Just look at the oil company!

What happened?

It used to be *give*. Now, it's *What can I get?* or *What can I take?*

Focused on the things outside,
Instead of the things inside.

People dying on the street, old people losing their homes,
Medicare is a joke.
It was to help the old folk.

There's nothing in this democracy to sell!
No money for those who served!
No food for those who are hungry!
No love for one another (those who shoot to kill)!
No help for those really in need.
No respect for the elders.

No God represented in the pledge,
Oh yes, and many more!
Someone has closed the door,
And our democracy is about to hit the floor—
Greed, money, and power!

Again, I stand up out of my chair and shout!
Does anyone care?
Is anyone there?

We need to take a stand on this promised land,
Or else our democracy will become a hypocrisy and slip into the sand.

But this is still, even now, in God's hand.

Yes, a democracy of hypocrisy to which I'm confined,
The democracy of supposed freedom a freedom that is limited to what we can and can't say.

Subjected at birth,
Demurred democracy, idolized democracy, yet all is a hypocrisy.

One that is policed not from within but outwardly to people who don't fit in.

Slammed, with the code of nine numbers, like a cow with a stamped ear!

Yes, this is our democracy,
One that tells me what to do.

It's our entire nation, one with which I'm through.
Angered, for it's a republic …
The people have no say.

Even the president has gone astray.
One nation under God no way, to my dismay!

What more is there to say …?

"All is frustration!" I let out with a mighty shout.

Democracy a hypocritical conspiracy of hypocrisy, in Calamity and strife, and who're people who aren't, and won't even *care*!

(Written on January 5, 2004)

Yet I fold my hands and cry, for what can I do
But preach to you? Yet I see people throw trash on the street and walk away like it was not there.

I shake and yell, "Wake up, wake up! Look outside yourself, and realize

We need to care!"
Yet my life is nothing but one.
So I scream again and try to stand on a democracy that is there!

(Added on October 18, 2005)

Depression Bites! But I pRaY!

"God give me the penitence to do your will and keep the peace!"

It bites at my legs ...
I struggle to run away from the thing that makes me feel pain.

I go through this even now.
I fall down ...

But I see others accomplish great things.
I want these things.

Yet my head swells,
and again, my mind, unfree,
It all feels messy,
and I begin to feel uneasy.
Unsteady ...
God, sometimes I feel unworthy.

Confusion and depression fill my head!

Sometimes, I feel then un-led.

You picked me!
Why, why could this be?
But you did, you did; in me you trust,
so yet I must ...

I must press on.
I must go on, for I have been called!

I cry.

Oh God, you have given me a task.
Sometimes, I lean on nothing, but I long to lean …
on you.

Lord, take this depression from me.

Yes, it's depression that tries to
grab,
bite,
gnaw,
hold,
and bind me into lack of thought.
It bites at my legs.

So I acknowledge
your idea; my expression comes together.

Brought to me by your power,
recognizing this, I don't let go of this expression,
realizing the truth,
recognizing the move in which you called me!

Now, with your power, when …
depression grabs,

I stab
back that pain and walk away.

Depression bites, but we fight!
Oh God, I thank you!

(Written on December 21, 2017)

Expressions

Is it me. Is it you?

Freedom is old freedom,
Will unfold.

Grabbing a towel from the bathroom,
I wipe my hands of the wetness that cleansed them.

Tossing the towel away, I pray
That someday, my life will be wiped away.

Every day the same, every day like the day before,
As I look out to the eastern shore,
I hope someday different comes knocking at my door!

Sometimes, I cry, sigh, beg, or fall into depression.
It's all an overwhelming sensation.

To understand to cope with life, to feel the anger, the frustration, or later the joy,
Sometimes, I want to destroy.

But inside me, I feel my expression become real.
I want to let others know.
I want them to see.

I want then *to feel*
My expression that is real.

A language that is beyond human intervention.
A strong sensation of later desperation.

Walking outside, I throw up my hands,
Looking up, realizing, and seeing that real language that is me.

I am put in bands, that is my hands,
By people who think they understand.

My mind wanders into that creative space
And spins into every race.

Black or white, you can't fight your inner sensation of you. Its every emotion all of a sudden comes alive. What are you going to do?

It's amazing to see that in me is an amazing realness that I can feel, one of utmost proclamation.
In that, it's all in one amazing realization, and that is an expression.

Author Description

Dorian Frost is a fiction and poetry author. In *A Feeling of Poetry*, he lures the reader in, not just with visuals, but with emotional realism as well. "A blast of a boom and crackle fills my ears as the sky pours down tears" is just a sample that truly awakens the senses. His skillful use of words is attributed to his lifelong writing. Dorian actually began creating other worlds and characters in the tenth grade. Many of these poetic themes come from life experiences expressed from the innermost realms of the soul. In other words, they are deep and can be mesmerizing.

People find Dorian's writing creative and nontraditional. Many find that once you pick up his writings, it is hard to put them down. "It is more than just a book; it's about the reader's experience," he would say.

Dorian was born and raised in the Washington, DC, area. He has always been interested in the simple things in life. He has a passion for nature and frequently goes camping. Lying underneath the stars has been a great source of inspiration for him. He is an author, artist, entrepreneur, and IT director. Dorian has a degree in IT, computer graphics, and multimedia design. He wants his readers to be on the lookout for *The Sacred Books of the Universe*, a release coming soon.

www.ingramcontent.com/pod-product-compliance
Lightning Source LLC
Chambersburg PA
CBHW071459070526
44578CB00001B/394